great songs of Lennon & McCartney

All musical compositions by John Lennon & Paul McCartney

Edited by **Milton Okun**

Associate Music Editor: **Dan Fox**   Text Editor: **Victoria Heller**

Quadrangle/The New York Times Book Co.

Second paperback edition, 1974

Library of Congress Catalog Card Number: 73-82491
International Standard Book Number: 0-8129-0509-1

With appreciation to the following music publishers:

NORTHERN SONGS LIMITED
12 Bruton Street
Mayfair
London W1X7 AH, England

MACLEN MUSIC, INC. & COMET MUSIC CORP.
6255 Sunset Boulevard
Hollywood, California 90028

GIL MUSIC CORP.
1650 Broadway
New York, N.Y. 10019

BEECHWOOD MUSIC CORP.
1750 North Vine Street
Hollywood, California 90028

ARDMORE & BEECHWOOD, LTD.
363 Oxford Street
London W1, England

DUCHESS MUSIC CORPORATION
445 Park Avenue
New York, N.Y. 10022

Photo Credits:
Thomson Newspapers, The New York Times, United Press International, CP,
The Associated Press & Rediffusion London Television House

Music Typography: **Music Art Co.**
Cover and Interior Design: **Jerry Lieberman**

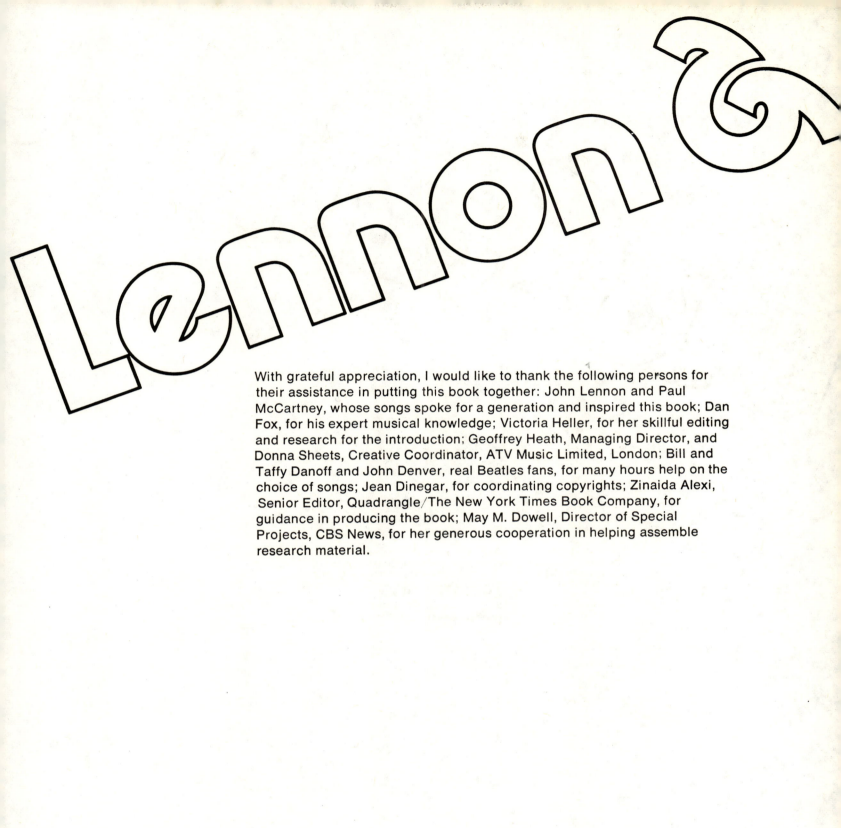

With grateful appreciation, I would like to thank the following persons for their assistance in putting this book together: John Lennon and Paul McCartney, whose songs spoke for a generation and inspired this book; Dan Fox, for his expert musical knowledge; Victoria Heller, for her skillful editing and research for the introduction; Geoffrey Heath, Managing Director, and Donna Sheets, Creative Coordinator, ATV Music Limited, London; Bill and Taffy Danoff and John Denver, real Beatles fans, for many hours help on the choice of songs; Jean Dinegar, for coordinating copyrights; Zinaida Alexi, Senior Editor, Quadrangle/The New York Times Book Company, for guidance in producing the book; May M. Dowell, Director of Special Projects, CBS News, for her generous cooperation in helping assemble research material.

To Rosemary

from Milt

Contents

Introduction	8
A Day In The Life	12
A Hard Day's Night	17
All My Loving	20
All You Need Is Love	23
And I Love Her	26
Back In The USSR	29
Baby You're A Rich Man	34
Because	38
Blackbird	42
Can't Buy Me Love	46
Carry That Weight	50
Come Together	52
Don't Let Me Down	55
Day Tripper	58
Eight Days A Week	60
Eleanor Rigby	64
For No One	66
Get Back	70
Give Peace A Chance	73
Girl	76
Golden Slumbers	80
Good Day Sunshine	83
Got To Get You Into My Life	88
Hello Goodbye	92

Help!	97
Here, There And Everywhere	100
Honey Pie	103
Hey Jude	108
I Am The Walrus	112
I Don't Want To See You Again	119
I Feel Fine	122
I Want To Hold Your Hand	126
If I Fell	130
In My Life	133
I'll Follow The Sun	136
I've Just Seen A Face	138
I'm A Loser	142
Let It Be	145
Lady Madonna	150
Love Me Do	154
Lucy In The Sky With Diamonds	158
Magical Mystery Tour	163
Michelle	166
Mother Nature's Son	170
Maxwell's Silver Hammer	174
Nowhere Man	177
Norwegian Wood	180
Ob-La-Di Ob-La-Da	182
Paperback Writer	188

Penny Lane	**191**
Rain	**196**
Ringo's Theme (This Boy)	**199**
Revolution	**204**
Rocky Raccoon	**208**
Sgt. Pepper's Lonely Hearts Club Band	**214**
She Came In Through The Bathroom Window	**219**
She Loves You	**222**
She's Leaving Home	**226**
Strawberry Fields Forever	**233**
The Ballad Of John & Yoko	**236**
The Fool On The Hill	**241**
Things We Said Today	**244**
Ticket To Ride	**248**
The Long And Winding Road	**252**
When I'm Sixty-Four	**255**
We Can Work It Out	**260**
With A Little Help From My Friends	**264**
World Without Love	**269**
Yellow Submarine	**272**
Yesterday	**275**
You Never Give Me Your Money	**278**
You've Got To Hide Your Love Away	**282**
Your Mother Should Know	**285**

> **"I always feel silly saying our songs will last."**
> **—Paul McCartney**

> **"When people ask to recreate the mood of the Sixties,**
> **they will play Beatle music."**
> **—Aaron Copland**

"The Beatles are coming!" It was a phrase spread five million times across the American countryside as an advance warning that an invasion was about to begin. Master publicist Brian Epstein, the Beatles' manager, had organized a publicity campaign that plastered buildings, fences and billboards with posters carrying likenesses of those who would become the four most wanted men in the musical world. Finally, in February of 1964—in flickering images of black and white television—Ed Sullivan brought the beat, the bangs and the brashness of John, Paul, George and Ringo to millions of Americans.

As the Beatles shook their moppet heads, parents gripped their chairs while their children were gripped by Beatlemania. In Los Angeles, an organization called Beatlesaniacs, Ltd. was formed to provide a cure for this new craze. Like the ten steps out of alcoholism, it suggested the following treatment:

Do not mention the word "Beatles" (or "beetles").
Do not mention such words as "luv," "fab," "gear," "ciggies."
Do not mention the word "Liverpool."
Do not mention the word "England."
Do not speak with an English accent.
Do not speak English.

Although parents and serious musicians did not take the Beatles' music seriously, there was a humor in the group that somehow justified all the publicity. They seemed to be looking at us looking at them, and they were laughing. They were somehow invulnerable. They seemed to be saying, "Take us or leave us, it's all a great big giggle."

In spite of their nose thumbing, there was an irresistible element of Cinderella about them: They were from lower-middle-class families in an un-chic section of England, Teddy boy takeoffs who would someday be decorated by the Queen. From poverty and the Liverpool slums, they would become multimillionaires and their songs would be recorded on over 545 million albums and singles around the world. In the 1960s, teenagers would lose their innocence, use drugs, create riots, run away from home, grow their hair, remove their underwear, drop out of school—and the Beatles would be blamed.

It wasn't all fads and fortune. In their decade together, the Beatles—John Lennon, Paul McCartney, George Harrison and Ringo Starr—made rock respectable, revolutionized the recording industry in general and the popular music industry in particular, set the precedent that a successful performer compose his own songs and brought a freedom to musical expression unprecedented in popular song. They took ideas from country and western, rhythm and blues, rock and roll. New musical terms were invented to describe their music: raga rock, baroque rock, white soul. They came up with nearly 200 songs of such beauty, irreverence, brutality, cynicism and humor that one prominent record reviewer and songwriter said, "I have it on the best authority that the Beatles do not write their own material. The fact is, they have a trained composer working for them in a small room in Mayfair who writes all their songs." They wrote songs of such variety that, rather than theorizing that one composer was writing for them, one might conclude that there were 200.

Eleven years after their first recording company audition, we realize that there was a promise in Epstein's publicity that even he could not have foreseen. The posters are gone, Beatlemania has disappeared along with the beer blast and the curfew, and the Beatles have reached their untrustworthy thirties. While memories of screaming teeny-boppers fade, the *enfants terribles* of rock have grown up and broken up. But their melodies linger on.

The early music of the Beatles was somewhat primitive, a little bit wicked, a whole lot exciting and uninhibited by the restraints of formal music training. What was unexpected was that they would evolve into serious musicians themselves. The genesis of their musical growth was the genius of one of the most successful and talented songwriting partnerships in the history of popular song—John Lennon and Paul McCartney, who wrote most of the songs performed by the Beatles.

Some critics have argued that, if they did not have a ghostwriter, they surely had a musical Svengali in the form of George Martin. Martin, a classically trained musician who had studied composition, conducting and oboe at the Guildhall School in London, headed Parlophone, the first recording company to sign the Beatles. He became their arranger and record producer. It has been said that the role of the producer changed with him, but I think the role of the recording artist changed as well. Before him, the producer functioned in two ways: Either he would approach an album with a concept in mind and mold his artists to fit that concept, or he would be a technological clerk attempting to get a pretty song, prettily sung, on tape with a minimum of expense and creative interference.

All this changed with the Beatles-Martin relationship, which introduced a new era in the recording studio. Martin's considerable expertise and background made it possible for the innate muscial vision of Lennon and McCartney to find a voice. None of the Beatles, except George, had any formal training and they were able to use Martin's experience in the expression of their limitless imaginations.

They profited from Martin's knowledge of the structure of classical music, a profound influence on their songs. One aspect of that influence was the use of modality, a feature of Western music that dates back to the Middle Ages. In the Lennon-McCartney songs, it appears as scale patterns slightly different from the standard major and minor scales most often heard in popular music. One hears almost subliminal notes, lowered sevenths, which are treated not as blue notes, but as they would sound in Elizabethan music. The most obvious example of the lowered seventh is in Paperback Writer. Another example of modality is Ticket To Ride, in which the F major-seventh is used instead of the expected D dominant seventh chord. Classical touches appear in many other songs, such as the trumpet solo in Penny Lane and the harpsichord in A Day In The Life.

When the Beatles went into a recording session, the studio was transformed into a musical laboratory with all four contributing to the experiment. The tape recording machine became a musical instrument. One could record an instrument at one speed and play it back faster or slower, reversed or distorted, and the alterations could be re-recorded. A single instrument could be recorded many times, the sound slightly altered each time and the tracks would be combined to give a totally new sound. High-frequency sounds, static, echo chambers, animal sounds and the spoken word could be used as well.

Beatle fans did their share of distorting also, an example of cultism in the extreme. A group of midwestern disc jockies had, in a horrendous hoax, determined that Paul McCartney was dead. One clue, it was said, was a line from Strawberry Fields Forever which, if played at 45 rpm instead of 33-1/3, stated clearly, "I buried Paul."

What was unprecedented about the Beatles' albums was their combinations of classical and electronic elements. But Lennon and McCartney expanded the horizons of popular songwriting as well. In the development of their songs, they often ignored the standard 32-bar pattern. Had they been formally trained, it would have been vastly more difficult to break such patterns. Instead, they had a kind of musical newspeak. An example of their flexibility of form is Day Tripper, which starts out as a standard, traditional 12-bar blues progression. But after 8 bars the pattern breaks into a new direction and the listener is tripped up, delighted by the unexpected. Another example of inventiveness is All You Need Is Love, which effortlessly changes in meter (4/4 to 3/4 or 3/4 to 4/4) in almost every bar of the song.

The Beatles had taken their music beyond the ordinary rock and roll context of guitar, bass guitar, drums and voice. By the time the public ear was trained to accept these technological innovations, Lennon and McCartney produced shocks with simplicity, using a string quartet in Yesterday that quietly punctuated the spareness of that ballad.

What is startling about Lennon and McCartney's music is its consistent growth. From sweaty sessions in a dank Liverpool nightclub to the surreal sophistication of their last album together, they never tried to repeat former successes. In the recording marketplace, it is a rule of thumb that once you do your thing successfully, you do it again, with minor changes. With Lennon and McCartney, there is a progression so that each song prepares us for the next. Listening to their songs at random, it is possible to place the period in which they were written. McCartney once said, "I always feel silly saying our songs will last. What I'm trying to say is that they may not be marvelous, but they're part of what's around at the moment."

What was around when Lennon and McCartney came together in 1962 was Chuck Berry and Elvis Presley, shouting with macho might to a hard rock beat. The Beatles imitated that sound in 12-hour nightclub sessions in Germany. Their performances, long on show and short on substance, still had the attraction of a scorn for the restraints of etiquette and musical form. While the lyrics were predictable—dealing with love, chauvinism, love, antiseptic sex and more love—the melodies of Lennon and McCartney were extraordinary. The sweep of the melody in All My Loving is close to that of a sixteenth-century art song. And I Love Her has a lovely melodic line; the melody of I Want To Hold Your Hand, when heard apart from its driving rock arrangement, can stand on its own. The melodies were good but the lyrics didn't match their quality.

By 1964—the year they met Bob Dylan—Lennon and McCartney's lyrics began to deal with ideas. The words became more abstract, more poetic, often wildly imaginative. They had a compassion, sensitivity and poignancy that has seldom been matched in popular music. Eleanor Rigby, written in 1965, contains a submerged passion that is reminiscent of Puccini. What is remarkable about the melody is that it is written with two chords, the tonic E minor and VI major C. There are no subdominant or dominant chords and no real cadence. It is the quiet tension of the lyrics, the outline of loneliness that suggests—but does not spell out—a story. The implications of "Waits at the window/Wearing the face that she keeps in a jar by the door" are breathtaking.

Norwegian Wood is another example of the fertility of this period in the Lennon-McCartney songs and it typifies their comic sense. The lyrics are about the humor of a one-night sexual stand. This song helped to popularize the use of the sitar and its simple harmonic pattern is striking. The first section of the song—a long, winding, descending melody is again based on only two chords.

Yesterday is also from this period and is probably the most popular song Lennon and McCartney ever wrote. In the United States alone, over 600 versions by various artists have been recorded. Having a melody that lends itself easily to a baroque treatment, it is comparable to the long, tugging melodic lines of Tschaikovsky's None But The Lonely Heart.

But the best was yet to come. The release of *Sgt. Pepper's Lonely Hearts Club Band* in 1967 marked the beginning of Lennon and McCartney's most creative work together. They had already proved that a lyric can sing the unsayable and sell and that a song need not be restricted to 32 bars. *Sgt. Pepper's* significance was that it marked the arrival of the recording studio as an art form. The live audience was replaced by the control room and it is no coincidence that by this time the Beatles had tired of touring. The energy expended on world tours was channeled into the studio and Lennon and McCartney wrote songs that could not be performed in the concert hall. *Meet The Beatles*, their first album, had taken 12 hours to record; *Sgt. Pepper* took four months. It synthesizes all the musical and electronic knowledge they had acquired, and the range of songs is a kaleidoscopic extravaganza unprecedented in the recording industry.

The compassion of Eleanor Rigby had become cynicism in She's Leaving Home, a bitter, ironic comment on middle-class values. When I'm Sixty-Four is a whimsical nugget of nostalgia and Lucy In The Sky With Diamonds, allegedly a tribute to LSD, is, for all its drug-connected controversy, freewheeling and exciting. But the high point of the album is the last cut, A Day In The Life. It might also be the high point in the creativity of Lennon and McCartney. The song, which was banned by the BBC because of the line, "I'd love to turn you on," is like the finest filmmaking, where what is not said is as important as what is; it has the feeling of worldweariness in which you are aware of life's horrors but it no longer matters: "I read the news today oh boy / About a lucky man who made the grade / And though the news was rather sad / Well I had just to laugh / He blew his mind out in a car / He didn't notice that the lights had changed . . ." The melody perks precariously beneath the lyrics like the score for a Fellini film, and the coda strains the listener's senses almost to the screaming point—the full orchestra playing a long, loud, electronically distorted glissando and resting on the final chord that slowly fades out over an agonizing 40 seconds.

The last six albums released by the Beatles used less and less electronic manipulation and were a return to basic music. My favorite song from this period is Golden Slumbers, a touching lullaby. The lyrics for this song are—with minor changes—taken from a sixteenth-century poem by Thomas Dekker called "Golden Slumbers Kiss Your Eyes." During this period, however, no less time was devoted to production. *The Beatles*, the double white album, took five months to produce. The impact of production techniques was so strong that the inherent beauty of their songs has been overlooked. Richard Goldstein wrote in *The New York Times*, "They are inspired posers, but we must keep our heads on their music, not their incarnations." Though sound and production greatly contribute to a song, the quality of its melody, harmony, rhythm and lyrics are more significant elements in the music of Lennon and McCartney, who—unlike other artists—do not need to disguise a lack of talent with sophisticated and elaborate sound and production techniques. The most astonishing thing about the songs of Lennon and McCartney is that their brilliance was profitable and that such enormous craftsmanship was phenomenally well received.

In the long run, however, if their songs are to last, they must be played by the layman, using his own voice, guitar, piano or organ. In this context it is important to forget the strong, vibrant performances of the Beatles and sing the songs, play the songs, read the songs. As they broke down barriers of form, so must the music lover dismiss the barriers of album production. It is possible to find new dimensions in these songs by playing them in new ways. She Loves You, for instance, can be played in a slow, ballad style that is more affecting to me than the almost wailing quality of the Beatles' driving rock version.

In the final analysis of the music of Lennon and McCartney, it is tempting to theorize about who contributed what in each particular song. I think this theorizing is unimportant, because their symbiotic creativity was more important than its separate parts. Moreover, the majority of their work was done on the spot, in the studio—a line here and a thought there—and put on tape.

Putting together this collection of 73 songs required some painful decisions since inevitably some superb songs had to be omitted. Still, these were selected as representative of the variety of the Lennon-McCartney nexus, a sampling from each stage of their writing together. The arrangements in this book are for piano, organ and guitar. The music has been compressed to two staves instead of the usual three, the upper staff for the vocal line and right-hand piano; the lower staff for left-hand and organ pedal notes. No attempt has been made to recreate the studio techniques used in the songs' album production.

What made the songs significant during the sixties was that emotions came out of the closet, not only in music but in all the arts. Lennon and McCartney's art told us about ourselves but they first prepared us for it. The hoopla that preceded their first U.S. tour prepared us for their act; their tours prepared us for their serious music. Because of their fame, each stage prepared us for the next, so that we swallowed it whole without thinking. But the history of music will offer evidence that their music survived the publicity, the elaborate recording techniques, the critics—even the Beatles themselves.

Milton Okun
London, England

August, 1973

A Day In The Life

Well   I   just   had   to   laugh - augh _____
They'd   seen   his   face   be - fore _____
But   I   just   had   to   look _____

I   saw   the   pho - to - graph - aph _____

No - bod - y   was   real - ly   sure   if   he   was   from   the House of   Lords _____

Hav - ing   read   the   book _____   I'd

love to turn _____ you _____ on.

Woke up got out of bed Dragged a

comb a-cross my head_ Found my way down stairs and drank a cup And

look - ing up I no - ticed I was late Found my

A Hard Day's Night

17

You know I feel al - right You know I

feel al - right.

1960 in Hamburg: Far left is Pete Best (later replaced by Ringo Starr); far right is Stu Sutcliffe (who died a short time afterward).

Shea Stadium N.Y.C. awaits the Beatles. (8/65)

All My Loving

Liverpool Town Hall. (7/64)

New York Times

All You Need Is Love

Noth-ing you can sing that can't be
No one you can save that can't be
Noth-ing you can see that is - n't

sung.   Noth-ing you can say but you can learn how to
saved.   Noth-ing you can do but you can learn how to
shown.   No-where you can be that is - n't where___ you're

play the game   It's eas - y (to 2nd verse)
be   you in time   It's eas - y (to chorus)
meant to be   It's eas - y (to chorus)

Tacet

Em   G   D/F♯ bass

Em   D7/A bass   G

D/F♯ bass   D7   D7

Chorus: (last time, repeat and fade)
G   A7sus4   D7

All   you need is love ____

all you need is love.___ all you need is love,___

___ love,___ love is all ___ you need.

D.S.

Thomson Newspapers

New York Times

And I Love Her

Gently, with a Latin feel

1. I give her all my love,⎯⎯ that's all I do,⎯⎯
2. She gives me ev-'ry-thing⎯⎯ and ten-der-ly,⎯⎯

And if you saw my love⎯⎯ you'd love her too,⎯⎯ I love her.
The kiss my lov-er brings⎯⎯ she brings to me,⎯⎯ And I love her.

*Guitarists: Capo up 3 frets.

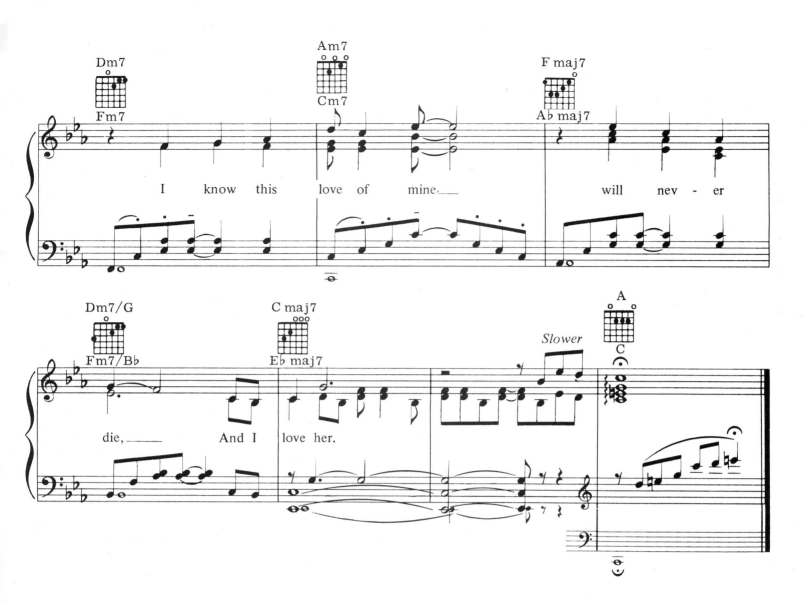

I know this love of mine will nev - er die, And I love her.

Back In The USSR

Moderate Boogie-Rock tempo

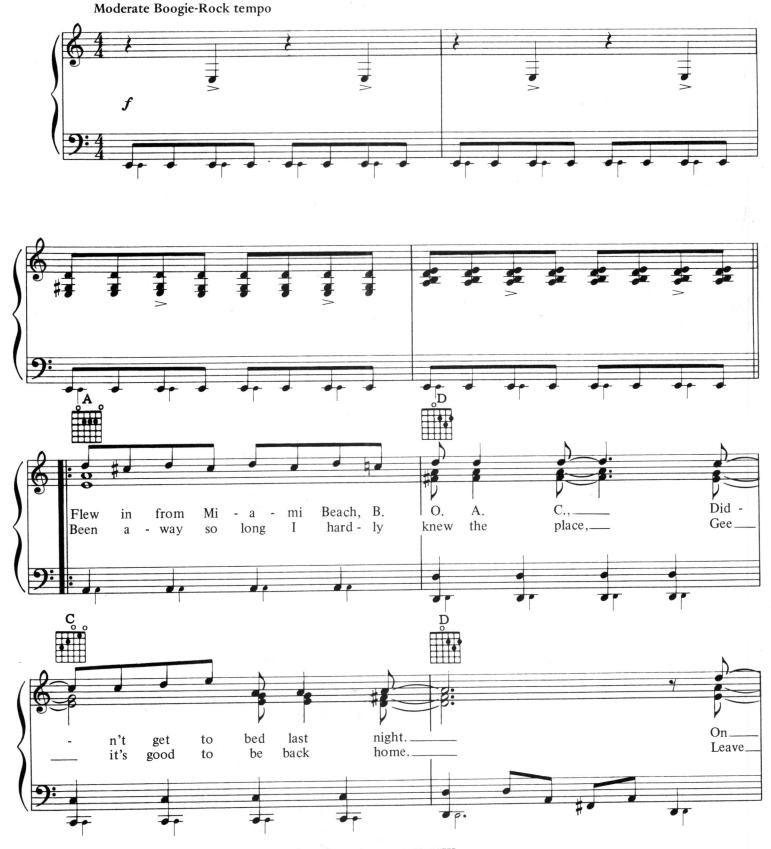

Flew in from Mi - a - mi Beach, B. O. A. C., ___ Did -
Been a - way so long I hard - ly knew the place, ___ Gee

- n't get to bed last night. ___ On
___ it's good to be back home. ___ Leave

the way the pa - per bag was on my knee,___ Man___
it till to - mor - row to un - pack my case,___ Hon -

___ I had a dread - ful flight. __ I'm back in the U. S. S. R.,___
- ey, dis - con - nect the phone. __

You don't know how luck - y you are,___ boy. __

Tacet

Back in the U. S. S. R. ___

mi - mi - mi - mi - mi - mi - mind._____ Show me round your snow peaked moun - tains way down south,___ Take ___ me to your dad - dy's farm.___ Let ___ me hear your ba - la - lai - kas ring - ing out,___ Come ___ and keep your com - rade warm.

Baby You're A Rich Man

far as the eye ___ can see. ___ How does it feel ___ to be

one of the beau - ti - ful peo - ple?

How of - ten have ___ you been there,
Tuned to a nat - u - ral E,

of - ten e - nough ___ to know. ___
hap - py to be ___ that way. ___

What did you see ___ when you were there ___ noth - ing that does ___ n't show..
Now that you've found ___ an - oth - er key ___ what are you going ___ to play? ___

G

Ba - by you're a rich man,

To Coda ✛

too. _____

D. S. al Coda 𝄋

C

✛ *Coda*

too. _____

Ba - by you're a rich man,

C

G

Repeat and fade

Ba - by you're a rich man,

Ba - by you're a rich man,

Because

Moderately slow

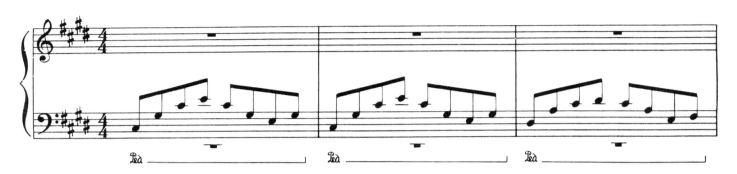

Ped. sim. throughout

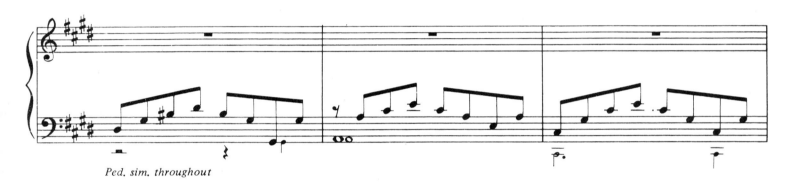

Ah, _____ Be -

C#m

D#m7–5

cause the world is round, it turns me on;
cause the wind is high, it blows my mind;

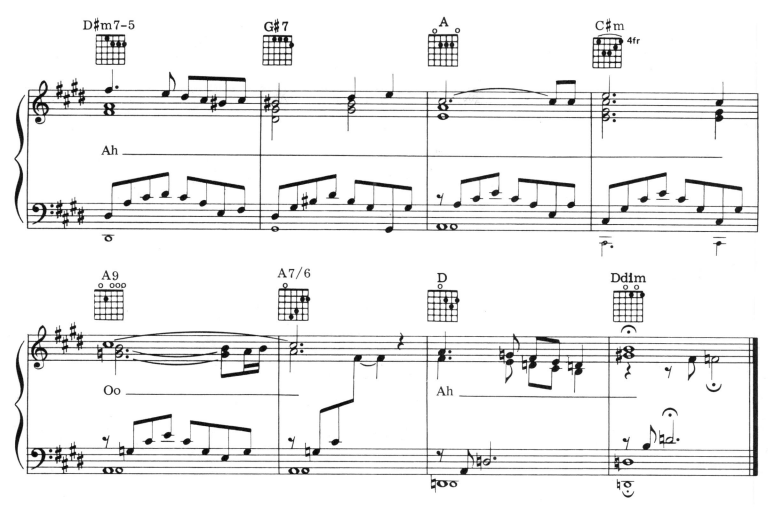

With Prince Phillip. (3/64)

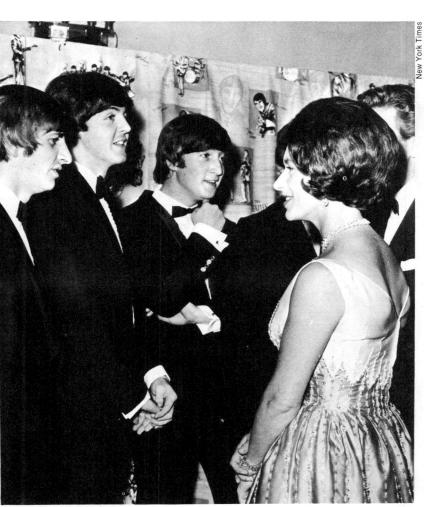

With Princess Margaret. (6/64)

Blackbird

* Guitarists: Play chords finger style.

free.   Black - bird, ___   fly, ___

Black - bird, ___   fly, ___   in - to the   light of a dark, black night. ___

Black - bird, ___ fly, ___ Black - bird, ___ fly, ___

___ in - to the light of a dark, black night. ___

molto rit.

a tempo

Black-bird sing-ing in the dead of night___ Take these brok-en wings_and learn to fly;

All your life___

You were on-ly wait-ing for this

mo-ment to a-rise,

You were on-ly wait-ing for this

mo-ment to ar-rive.

slower

Can't Buy Me Love

makes you feel al - right.
got I'll give to you.

For I don't care too

much for mon - ey, for mon - ey can't buy me love. I'll

can't buy me love, ev -

- 'ry - bod - y tells me so. Can't buy me love,

no no no____ no!

Say you don't need no dia - mond rings____ and I'll be sat - is - fied,____

Tell me that you want those kind ____ of things____ that mon - ey just can't buy.__

Break

I don't care too much for mon - ey,

mon - ey can't buy me love.___ Can't buy me love ___

___ love ___ can't buy me love.___

John's Rolls-Royce.

Carry That Weight

Come Together

Moderately slow, with a double-time feeling

I know ___ you, you ___ know me. ___
feet down be-low his knee. ___
one and one and one is three ___

One thing I can tell you is you got to be free. ___
Hold you in his arm-chair, you can feel his dis-ease. ___
Got to be good look-ing 'cause he so hard to see. ___

Come to-geth-er, ___ right now, ___ o-ver me. ___

After last verse D.C. and fade

54

Don't Let Me Down

Special note:
This song was recorded by the Beatles in the key of E, ½ step higher than this arrangement. Pianists may play with the record by mentally changing the key signature to four sharps.
Guitarists should capo up three frets for the written key, four frets if they wish to play with the record.

(May be sung an 8va higher)

Slowly

mf

Don't let me down,

Don't let me down, _____

Don't let me

down, _____

Don't let me down. _____

Tacet

No - bod - y ev - er loved me like she does, oo she
And from the first time that she real - ly done me, oo she

Don't let me down. _____ I'm in love for the first

_____ time. _____ Don't you know it's gon - na last.

It's a love that lasts for - ev - er, _____ It's a love that had no

past. Don't let me down. _____

Trip-per,   one - way tick - et, yeah.___
Trip-per,   one - way tick - et, yeah.___
Trip-per,   Sun - day driv - er, yeah.___

It took me

so___   long___ to find out,   and I found out.

Play 3 times

mf

Repeat and fade

Day Trip-per,   Day Trip-per, yeah!

Eight Days A Week

not e - nough to show I care. ___ { Ooh I need your
Love you ev - 'ry

love, babe, ___ guess you know it's true. ___ Hope you need my
day, girl, ___ al - ways on my mind. ___ One thing I can

love, babe, ___ just like I need you. ___ } Hold me, ___
say, girl, ___ love you all the time. ___ }

love me, ___ Hold me, ___ love me. I

ain't got noth-in' but love, babe,— eight days a week.—

Eight days a week.— Eight days a week.—

Paul with Diana Ross and The Supremes. (1/68)

Eleanor Rigby

Moderately, with a steady beat

Ah_____ look at all_____ the lone-ly peo - ple!_____

Ah_____ look at all_____ the lone-ly peo - ple!_____

1. El - ea - nor Rig - by, picks up the rice___ in the church___ where a wed - ding has been,_
2. Fa - ther Mc Ken - zie, writ - ing the words_ of a ser - mon that no_____ one will hear,_
3. El - ea - nor Rig - by, died in the church___ and was bur - ied a - long___ with her name,

lives in a dream.___
no one comes near.___
no - bod - y came.___

Waits at the win - dow,
Look at him work - ing,
Fa - ther Mc Ken - zie,

For No One

is dead; you think she needs you. And in her
he's gone; she does-n't need him.

Your day breaks, your mind aches, there will be times

when all the things she said will fill your head; you

won't for-get her. And in her eyes you see

noth - ing _____ no sign of love be - hind the tears _____

cried for no _____ one a love that

should have last - ed years. _____ *rit.*

Get Back

-son, Ar - i - zo - na, for____ some Cal - i - for - nia grass.
____ she's got it com - ing, But____ she gets it while she can.

Get back!____   Opt. fill   Get back!____   Get back

____ to where you once be - longed.____   Get back!____   Get back!

Get back____ to where you once be - longed.____   *(Get back, Jo Jo)*

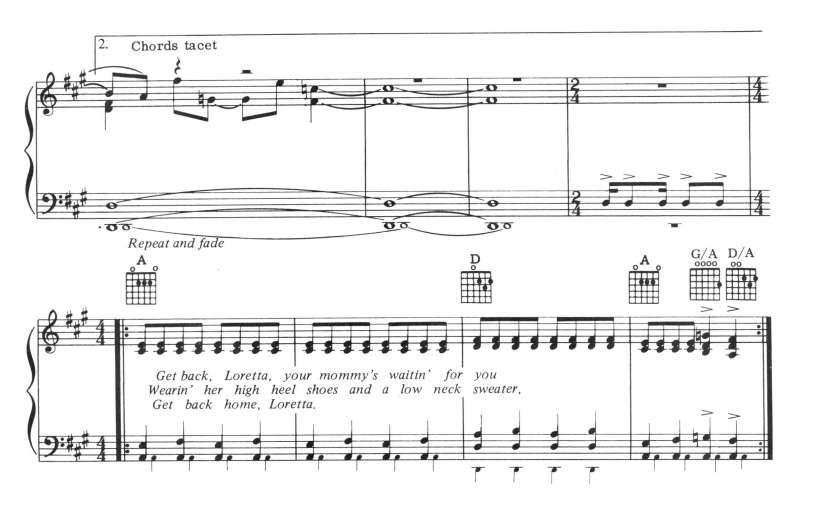

Repeat and fade

Get back, Loretta, your mommy's waitin' for you
Wearin' her high heel shoes and a low neck sweater,
Get back home, Loretta.

New York Times

Give Peace A Chance

F/Gbass   Em/Gbass   **G7**   **C**

— is give peace___ a chance.

1.
C' mon,

2.
Let me tell you now,

3.
Oh, let's stick to it,

4.   *D.S. and fade* 𝄋
All we___ are

Girl

* Guitarists capo up 3 frets

Golden Slumbers

Gold - en slum - bers fill your eyes.

Smiles a - wake you when___ you___ rise; Sleep pret-ty dar -

- ling, do not cry, And I will sing a lull-a-

by.___ Once, there was a way___ to get back

Dm7

home- ward. —

G7

Once, there was a way —

C **Em**

to get back home. Sleep pret - ty dar

Am

- ling, do not

Dm9

cry,

G7

And I will sing a lull - a -

C

by. —

New York Times

Good Day Sunshine

lie   be - neath a   shad - y tree   I   love her and she's

lov - ing me. ____ She feels good, ____   she knows she's look - ing fine,

I'm   so proud to know that   she is mine. ____   Good   day ____   sun -

- shine, ____   Good   day ____   sun -   shine, ____

Got To Get You Into My Life

-den - ly see___ you. Ooh,_____ did I tell___ you I need___ you

ev - 'ry sin - gle day of my life?_____

2. You did - n't run, you did - n't lie you knew I want - ed just to hold you.___
3. What can I do, what can I be, when I'm with you I want to stay there,___

And had you gone you knew in time we'd meet a - gain for I'd have
___ If I'm true I'll nev - er leave and if I do I know the

Got to get you in - to my life!

With Prime Minister Harold Wilson. (3/64)

New York Times

Hello Goodbye

I don't_ know why you say good-bye_ I say hel-lo_

Why why why

why why why_ do you say_ good-bye_ good-bye_

Hel-lo_ hel-lo_____ I don't_ know

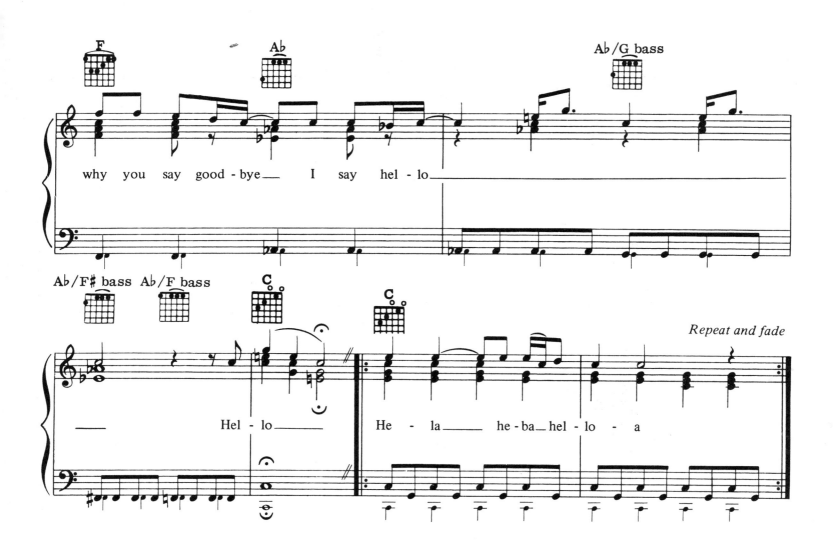

why you say good-bye___ I say hel - lo___

Hel - lo___ He - la___ he - ba___ hel - lo - a

Repeat and fade

Help!

Here, There And Everywhere

There,   run-ning my hands__ thru her hair__

both of us think-ing how good____ it can be;____

Some-one is speak-ing but she does-n't know__ he's there.__   I want her

ev-'ry-where   and if she's be-side me I know I need nev-er care.

But to love her is to meet her ev-'ry-where, know-ing that love__ is to share;__

Each one be-liev-ing that love__ nev-er dies,__ watch-ing her eyes__ and hop-

-ing I'm al-ways there.__ I want her To be there__

and ev-'ry-where,__ here, there and ev-'ry-where.__

Honey Pie

Hon - ey Pie,___ you are driv - ing me fran - tic.___
Hon - ey Pie,___ you are mak - ing me cra - zy,___

Sail a - cross___ the At - lan - tic, to be where you be - long___
I'm in love___ but I'm la - zy, so won't you please come___ home

Hon - ey Pie, come back to ___ me.

Come, come back to me, Hon - ey Pie. Ha ___

ha ha, Oo

Oo Hon - ey Pie, come

back.

Hey Jude

* Guitarists: Capo up 3 frets.

Repeat and fade

to make it bet - ter, bet -ter, bet - ter, bet - ter, bet - ter, bet - ter, Oh

Da da da da da da da da da da Hey Jude.

I Am The Walrus

THE TAMING OF THE SHREW
by William Shakespeare

Dramatis Personae

Baptista Minola, of Padua, father of Kate and Bianca

Kate, the shrew

Bianca

Petruchio, of Verona, suitor of Kate

Lucentio (Cambio) ⎫

Gremio, a pantaloon ⎬ suitors of Bianca

Hortensio (Litio) ⎭

Vincentio, of Pisa, father of Lucentio

A Pedant (impersonating Vincentio)

Tranio (later impersonating Lucentio) ⎫

Biondello ⎬ servants of Lucentio

Grumio

Curtis ⎫

Nathaniel, Nicholas ⎬ servants of Petruchio

Joseph, Philip, Peter ⎭

Scene--Padua; the country near Verona

they fly_____   I'm   cry - ing_____

Sit - ting on a corn - flake_____   wait - ing for the van to come_____
Yel - low mat - ter cus - tard_____   drip - ping from a dead dog's eye_____

Cor - por - a - tion tee shirt, stu - pid blood - y Tues - day man_____
Crab - a - lock - er fish - wife por - no - graph - ic priest - ess boy_____

_____ you been a naught - y boy_____ you let your face grow long_____   I am the
_____ you been a naught - y girl_____ you let your knick - ers down_____

egg-man   Oh they are the egg-men   Oh   I am the wal-rus   Goo goo g' joob

1. Mis-ter cit-y p'lice-man sit-ting   pret-ty lit-tle p'lice-men in a row___

___   See how they fly like Lu-cy in the sky see how___

___ they run___   I'm cry - ing___   I'm cry -

ing I'm cry - ing I'm cry - - -

ing   effects

Sit - ting in an Eng - lish gar - den wait-ing for the sun____ If the sun don't come____

____ you get a tan from stand - ing in the Eng - lish rain____ I am the

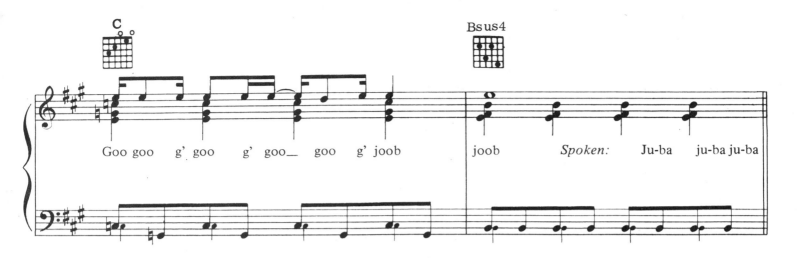

Goo goo g' goo g' goo____ goo g' joob   joob   *Spoken:* Ju-ba ju-ba ju-ba

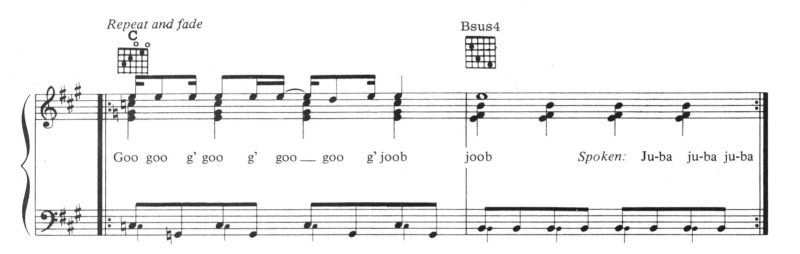

Repeat and fade

Goo goo g' goo g' goo ____ goo g' joob   joob   *Spoken:* Ju-ba ju-ba ju-ba

With Maharishi Mahesh Yogi. (8/67)

I Don't Want To See You Again

You hid the light ___ of ___ day. I did-n't have to play___ ___ at be - ing brok - en - heart - ed. ___ I know that lat - er on af - ter love's been and gone, I'll still hear some - one say

120

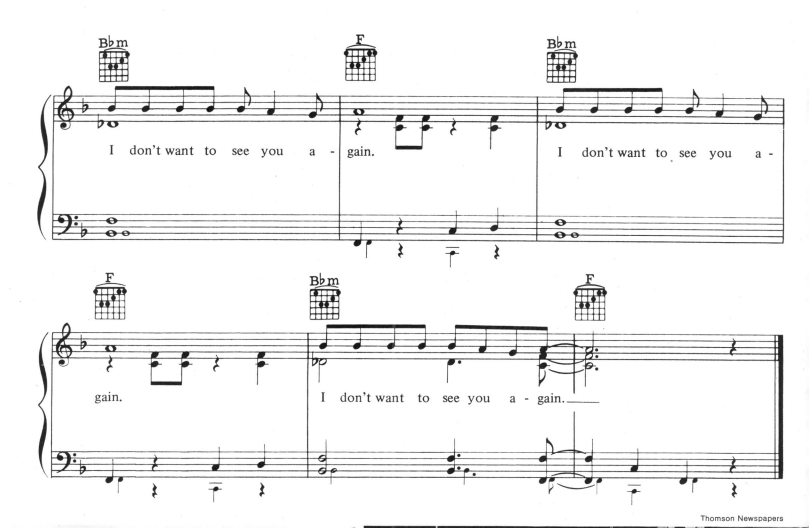

I don't want to see you a - gain.

I don't want to see you a -

gain.

I don't want to see you a - gain.____

Accepts Grammy award for "Let It Be". (3/71)

LOVE L'AMOUR IHR LO

IS C'EST BRAUCHT QUE

YO POU ALS ES

NEED VOUS LIEBE AMOR

I Feel Fine

Bright rock

Ba - by's good to me, — you know, — she's hap - py as can be, — you know, — she said so.

I'm in love__ with her and I__ feel__ fine.__

Ba - by says she's mine,__ you know,__ she tells me all the time,__

__ you know,__ she said so.

I'm in love__ with her and I__ feel__ fine.__

A Hard Day's Night.

I Want To Hold Your Hand

128

I want to hold your hand,

I want to hold your hand.

Thomson Newspapers

Thomson Newspapers   Thomson Newspapers

If I Fell

very start that you would love me more than
love you, too. Oh, you please don't hurt my pride like

her.

If I

'Cause I

could-n't stand the pain. And I would be

sad if our new love was in vain. So I

In My Life

*Guitarists capo up 1 fret

dead__ and__ some__ are__ liv - ing, In my life__ I've loved them all.__

know I'll of - ten stop and think a - bout them In my life__ I'll love you more.__

In 18th Century style

organ pedal tacet

Though I

know I'll nev - er lose af - fec - tion__ for peo - ple and things__ that

134

I'll Follow The Sun

I've Just Seen A Face

I've just seen a face I can't for - get the time___ or place where we just

met. She's just the girl___ for me and I___ want all the world to see___ we've

met. Mm mm mm mm___ mm.___

Had it been___ an-oth-er day___ I might have looked the
I have nev-er known the like___ of this I've been a-

oth-er way___ and I'd have nev-er been___ a-ware.___ But
lone and I___ have missed things and kept out___ of sight.___ For

as it is I'll dream of her___ to-night,___
oth-er girls were nev-er quite___ like this,___ Da da

da da da da.___ Fall - ing,___ yes, I am

fall - ing,___ And she keeps call - ing___ me back a -

1.
gain.

2.
gain.

Fall - ing,____ yes, I am fall - ing,____

And she keeps call - ing____ me back a -

Chords tacet

gain._____

I'm A Loser

Am7 **D7** **G**

some-one who's near ___ to me. I'm a los- -

Play 3 times

Em **Am7** **F** **D7** **G**

er, and I'm not what I ap-pear ___ to be. ___

Rehearsing for "A Midsummer Night's Dream" TV show. (4/64)

Rediffusion

Thomson Newspapers

144

Let It Be

Slowly

standing right in front of me Speaking words of wisdom,} Let it
still a chance that they will see There will be an answer,} Let it

be. let it be, let it be, let it be,

let it be, {Whisper words of wisdom, Let it be.
{There will be an answer, Let it be.

2. And when Let it be

let it be, ___ let it be, ___ let it be, ___

Whis - per words_ of wis - dom, let it be._

And when___ the night_ is cloud - y there is

149

Lady Madonna

Brightly, with a beat

Lady Ma - don - na,   chil - dren at your feet,___
Lady Ma - don - na,   ba - by at your breast,___

Won - der how you man - age to make___ ends   meet.___
Won - der how you man - age to feed___ the   rest.___

152

Love Me Do

Moderate rock

mf

Love, love me do, you know I love you,

I'll al - ways be true, so

Lucy In The Sky With Diamonds

slow - ly   a   girl   with   ka - lei - do - scope   eyes.____
flow - ers   that grow   so   in - cred - i - bly   high.____

Bb

____   Cel - lo - phane
____   News - pa - per

mf

F6

flow - ers   of   yel - low   and   green   tow - er - ing
tax - is   ap -   pear   on   the   shore   wait - ing   to

Bb   C9

o - ver   your   head____   Look   for   the
take you   a - way____   Climb   in   the

Chords tacet

Pic - ture your - self on a train in a sta - tion with

plas - ti - cine por - ters with look - ing glass ties.

Sud - den - ly some - one is there at the turn - stile the

girl with ka - lei - do - scope eyes. _____

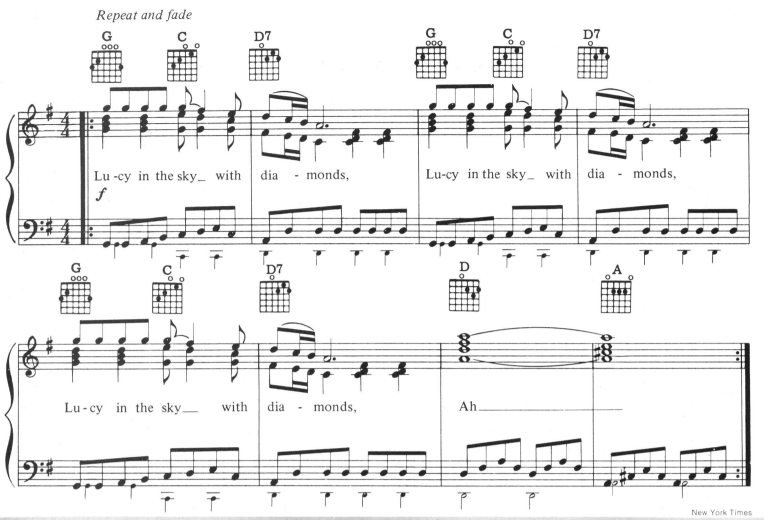

Magical Mystery Tour

With a beat (in 2)

Roll up, roll up for the Magical Mystery Tour. Step right this way.

Roll up,_____ Roll up___ for the mys-

- te - ry tour.___ Roll up,_____

Roll up___ for the mys - te - ry tour.___

(1.3.) Roll up,___ and that's an
(2.) Roll up, we've got ev - 'ry-

Michelle

* Guitarists: Capo up 5 frets. (For recorded key, capo up 8 frets.)

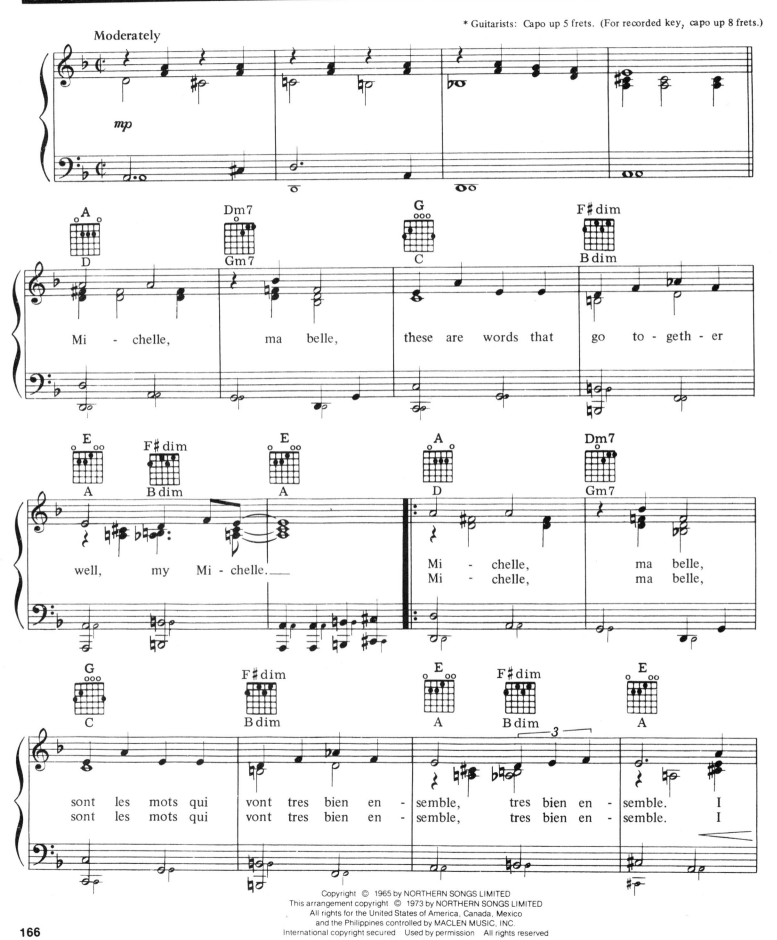

I want you, I want you, I want you, I think you know by

now, I'll get to you some - how.___ Un - til I do, I'm

tell - ing you, so you'll un - der - stand: Mi - chelle,

ma belle, sont les mots qui vont tres bien en - semble, tres bien en-

Mother Nature's Son

173

Maxwell's Silver Hammer

Clang! Clang! Max - well's   sil - ver ham - mer made   sure   that she was   dead.
Clang! Clang! Max - well's   sil - ver ham - mer made   sure   that she was   dead.
Clang! Clang! Max - well's   sil - ver ham - mer made   sure   that he was   dead.

Sil - ver

ham - mer.

Nowhere Man

Scene from *Help!*

"I once had a girl, or should I say she once had me"

Norwegian Wood

Moderately

181

Ob-La-Di Ob-La-Da

* Guitarists capo up one fret.

la how their life goes on. ____

In a cou-ple of years they have built a home ____

____ sweet home. ____

with a cou-ple of kids run-ning in the yard ____

184

eve - ning she still sings it with the band.____
eve - ning she's a sing - er with the band.____

Ob - la - di____

____ Ob - la - da____ life goes on____ bra____ la____

____ la how the life goes on.____

Ob - la - di____

____ Ob - la - da____ life goes on____ bra____ la____ la how the

186

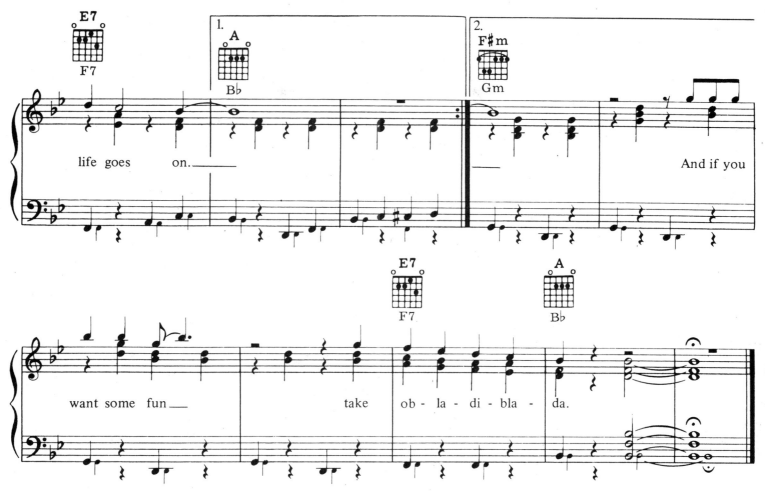

New York Times

Paperback Writer

Bright Rock

want to be a pa-per-back writ-er,_____ pa-per-back
want to be a pa-per-back writ-er,_____ pa-per-back

writ-er._____ It's the dirt-y sto-ry of a dirt-y man,__and his
writ-er._____ If you real-ly like it you can have the rights,_ it could

cling - ing wife does - n't un - der-stand. His son is work-ing for the
make a mil-lion for you o - ver - night. If you must re - turn it you can

Dai - ly Mail;_ It's a stead - y job__ but he wants to be a pa-per-back
send it here,_ But I need a break_ and I want to be a pa-per-back

189

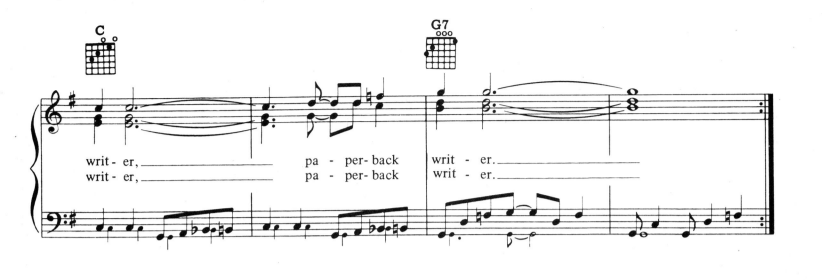

writ - er,_____ pa - per-back writ - er._____
writ - er,_____ pa - per-back writ - er._____

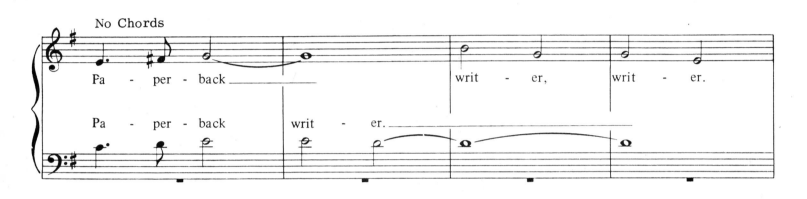

No Chords

Pa - per-back _____ writ - er, writ - er.
Pa - per-back writ - er._____

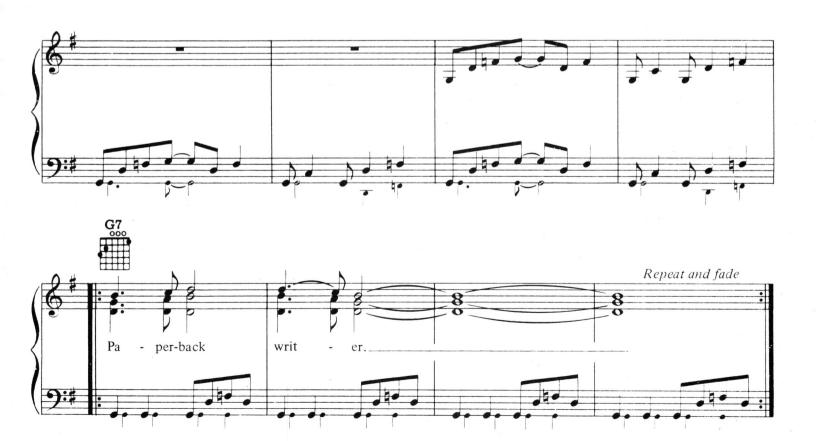

G7

Repeat and fade

Pa - per-back writ - er._____

190

Penny Lane

Moderate barrel-house tempo

Pen - ny Lane: There is a bar-ber show-ing pho-to-graphs___ of ev-'ry

head he's had the pleas-ure to know.____ And all the peo-ple that come and go

___ stop and say hel - lo. On the

cor - ner is a bank-er with a mo-tor car,___ The lit-tle chil-dren laugh at him be-hind his
Lane there is a fire-man with an hour-glass,__ And in his pock-et is a por-trait of the

back, _____ And the bank-er nev-er wears a "mac" _____ in the
Queen. _____ He likes to keep his fire _____ en - gine clean, _____ it's a

pour - ing rain, ver - y strange. Pen - ny Lane is in my ears _____ and in my eyes, _____
clean ma - chine. _____ Pen - ny Lane is in my ears _____ and in my eyes, _____

There be - neath the blue _____ sub - urb - an skies. _____
_____ A four of fish _____ and fin - ger pies _____

_____ I sit, and mean - while, back in Pen - ny
_____ in sum - mer. Mean - while, back be - hind the

poco rubato

shel - ter in the mid - dle of the round a - bout,___ a pret - ty nurse is sell - ing pop - pies from a

tray.___ And tho' she feels as if she's in a play,___ she is

an - y - way. Pen - ny Lane: The bar - ber shaves an - oth - er
Rhythmically, as before

cus - tom - er,___ We see the bank - er sit - ting, wait - ing for a trim.___ And then the

fire - man rush - es in _____ from the pour - ing rain, ver - y

strange.   Pen - ny   Lane   is   in   my   ears ____   and   in   my   eyes, ____

There   be - neath   the   blue ____   sub - urb - an   skies. ____   I   sit   and

mean - while   back...   Pen - ny   Lane   is   in   my   ears ____   and   in   my   eyes, ____

There be-neath the blue___ sub-urb-an skies.

Pen-ny Lane.___

Without slowing down

Rain

C **D** **G**

show you that when it starts to rain
hear me that when it rains and shines it's

C **D** **G** **C**

ev-'ry-thing's the same. I can show you.___ I can
just a state of mind. Can you hear me?___ Can you

G

show you.
hear me?

1.
you.

2.
me?

HAIR PEACE.

BED PEACE.

Peace protest.

Ringo's Theme (This Boy)

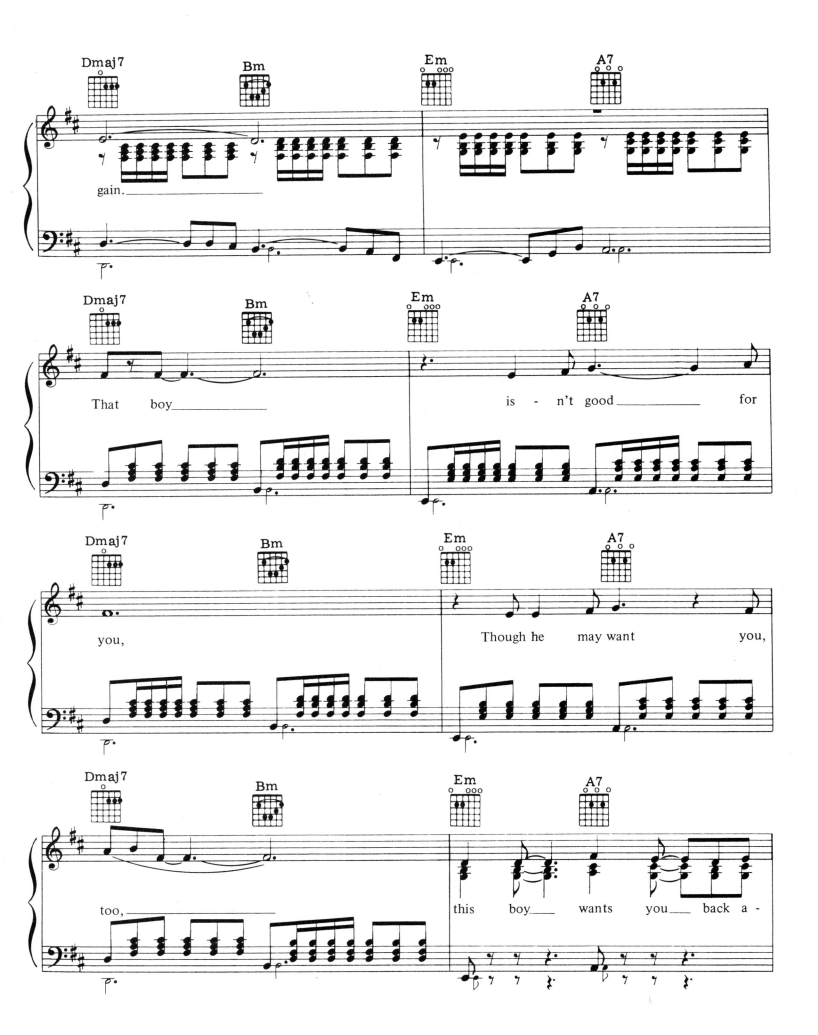

gain._____ Oh, and_____

this boy___ would be hap-py___ just to

love___ you.___ But oh, my!_____ Oh,____

that boy___ won't be hap-py___

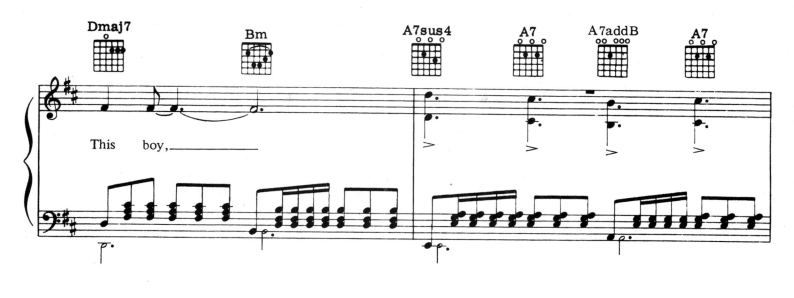

This boy,_____

Repeat and fade

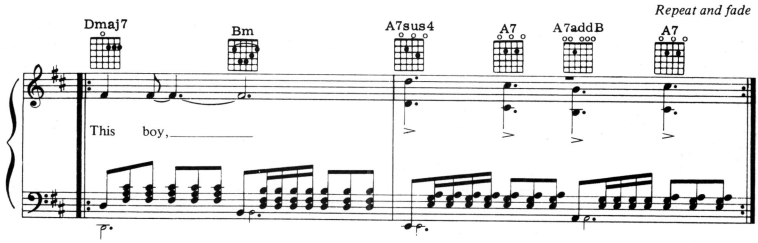

This boy,_____

Revolution

Moderate Tempo

world.
plan.
head.

You tell me that it's e - vo - lu -
You ask me for a con - tri - bu -
You tell me it's the in - sti - tu -

- tion,_____ Well _____ you know,_____
- tion,_____ Well _____ you know,_____
- tion,_____ Well _____ you know,_____

We all want _____ to change the world._____
We're all do - ing what we can._____
You bet-ter free _____ your mind in - stead._____

But when you talk a - bout de - struc - tion,_____
But if you want mon-ey for peo-ple with minds that hate,_____
But if you go car - ry-ing pic-tures of Chair - man Mao,_____

Don't   you know   that you   can count me   out.___
All   I can tell you is broth-er you   have to   wait.___
You ain't going to make it with an - y -one   an - y - how.___

Don't you know it's gon - na   be ___   al - right, ___

al - right, ___   al - right.

You
You

Al - right, _____ al - right, _____ al - right,

al - right, _____ al - right, _____ al - right,

al - right, _____ al - right.

"Her name was Magill but she called herself Lil, but ev'ryone knew her as Nancy"

Rocky Raccoon

Moderately

Am7 — D7

Spoken: Now somewhere in the Black Mountain hills of Dakota there lived a
He said, "I'm going to get that boy."

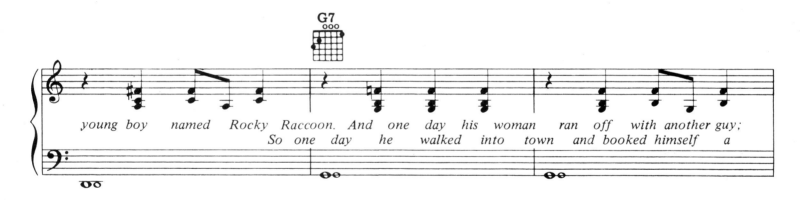

G7

young boy named Rocky Raccoon. And one day his woman ran off with another guy;
So one day he walked into town and booked himself a

C — C/B bass

Hit Rocky in the eye,
room in a local

Rocky didn't like that.
saloon.

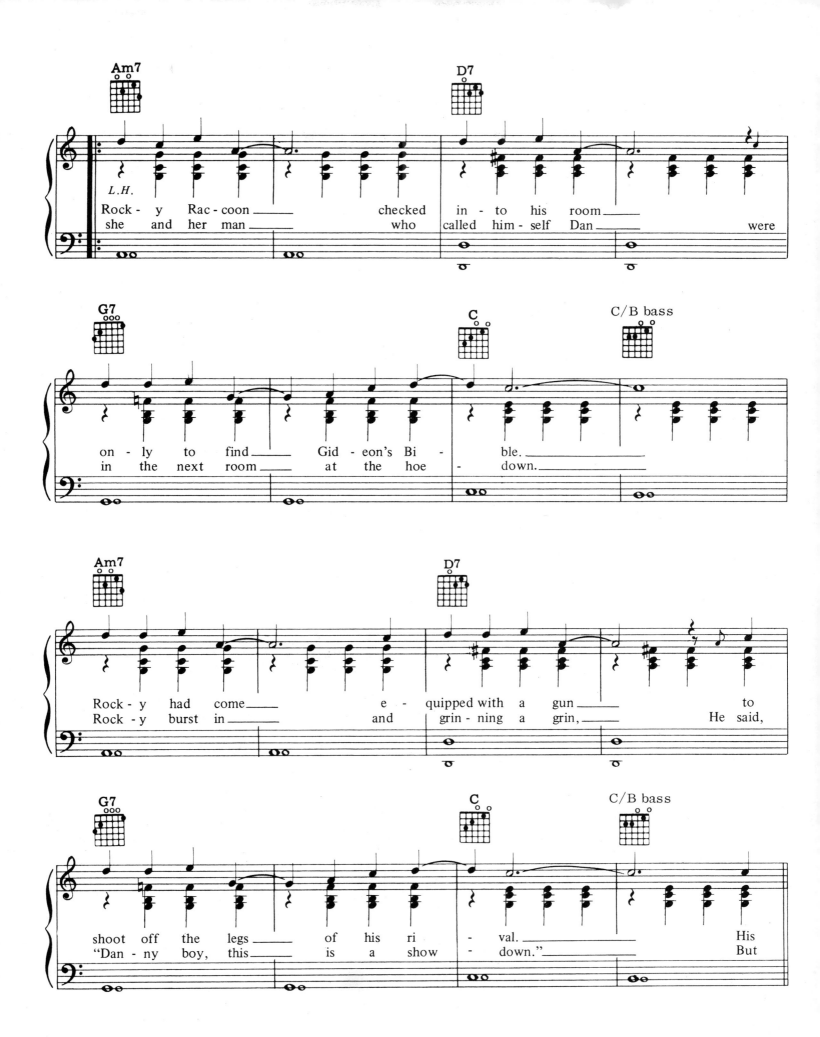

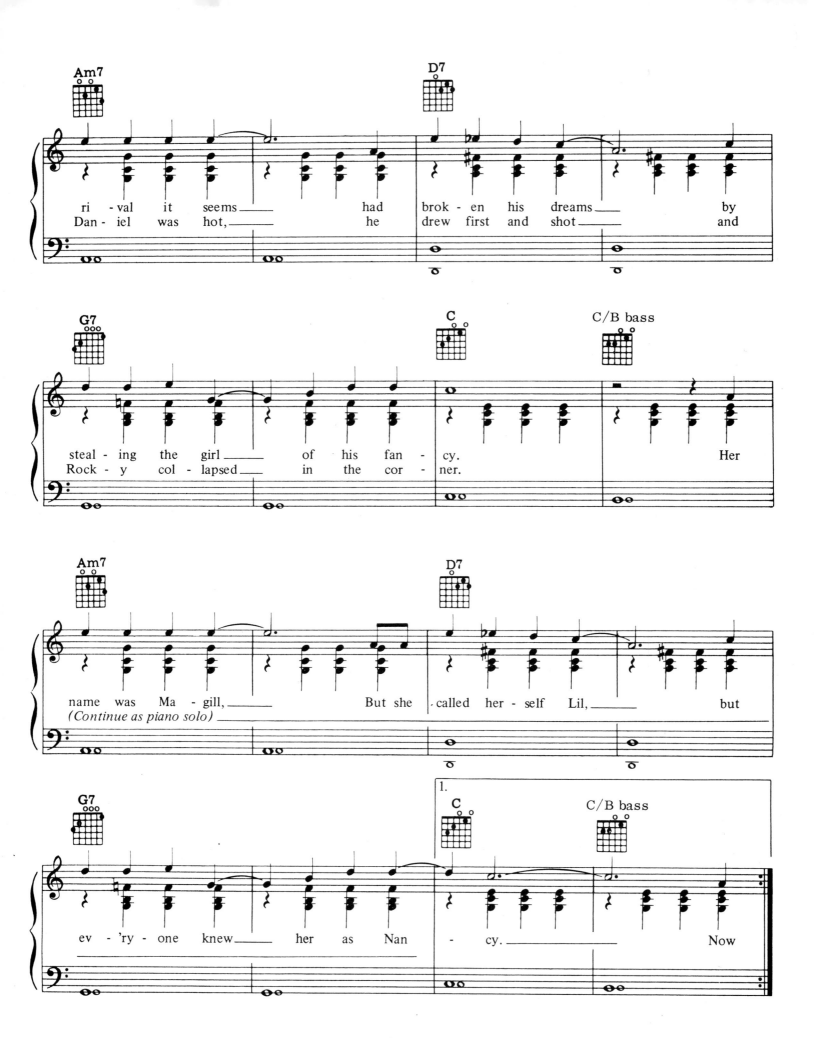

ri - val it seems _____ had brok - en his dreams _____ by
Dan - iel was hot, _____ he drew first and shot _____ and

steal - ing the girl _____ of his fan - cy.
Rock - y col - lapsed _____ in the cor - ner. Her

name was Ma - gill, _____ But she called her - self Lil, _____ but
(Continue as piano solo) _____

ev - 'ry - one knew _____ her as Nan - cy. _____ Now

1.

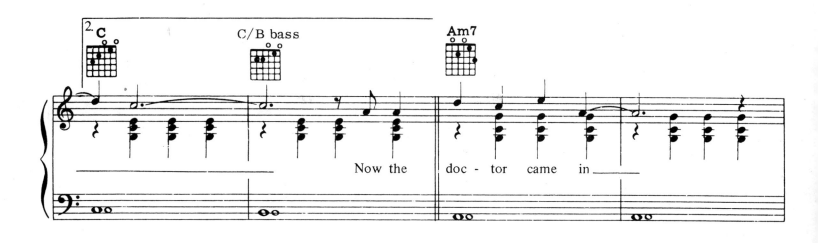

Now the doc - tor came in

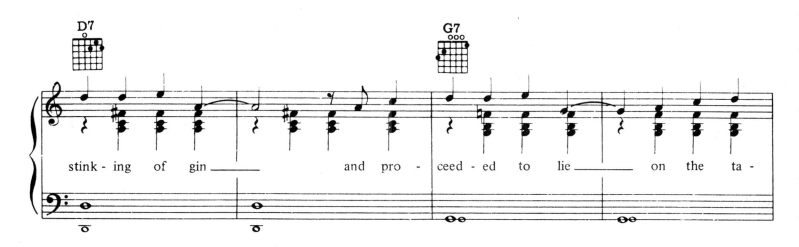

stink - ing of gin ___ and pro - ceed - ed to lie ___ on the ta-

ble. He said, "Rock - y, you met ___ your match," And Rock - y

said, "Doc, it's on - ly a scratch, ___ And I'll be bet - ter, I'll be bet - ter Doc, as soon ___ as I'm

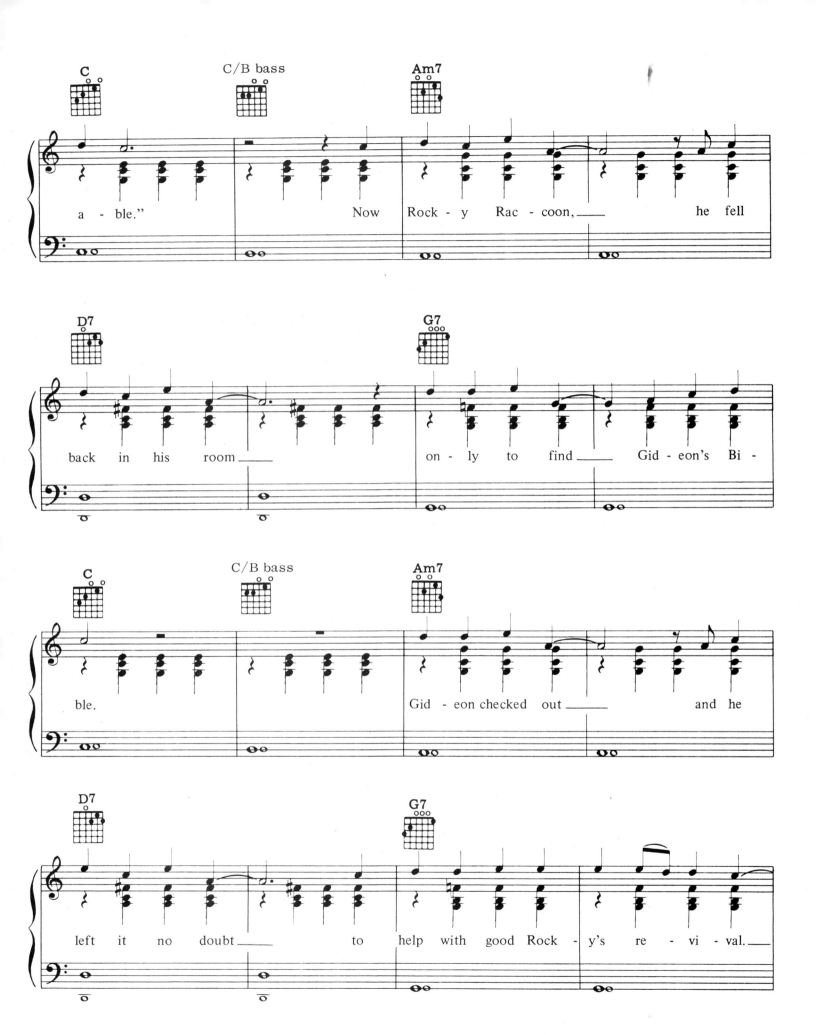

a-ble." Now Rock-y Rac-coon,____ he fell

back in his room____ on-ly to find____ Gid-eon's Bi-

ble. Gid-eon checked out____ and he

left it no doubt____ to help with good Rock-y's re-vi-val.____

Barrelhouse style (♩♩♩♩ to be played like ♩. ♪ ♩. ♪)

Sgt.Pepper's Lonely Hearts Club Band

215

Bb 6fr · F 8fr · C 8fr · G 3fr

Ser - geant Pep - per's Lone - - ly Hearts___ Club Band,___ Sit
Ser - geant Pep - per's Lone - - ly Hearts___ Club Band,___ We're

A7 5fr · D7 3fr · C 8fr · G 3fr

back and let the eve - ning go. ___ Ser - geant Pep - per's Lone - ly, Ser -
sor - ry but it's time to go. ___ Ser - geant Pep - per's Lone - ly, Ser -

A7 5fr · C 8fr

- geant Pep - per's Lone - ly, Ser - geant Pep - per's Lone - ly Hearts
- geant Pep - per's Lone - ly, Ser - geant Pep - per's Lone - ly Hearts

C/D bass 5fr · G 3fr · 1. C 8fr

Club Band. ___ It's won - der - ful to be here, it's
Club Band. ___

216

certain - ly a thrill, You're such a love - ly au - di - ence, we'd

like to take you home with us, we'd love to take you home. I don't

Ser - geant Pep - per's Lone - ly Hearts Club Band,___ We'd

like to thank you once a - gain.___ Ser - geant Pep - per's one and on - ly

She Came In Through The Bathroom Window

Moderately slow

Tues - days on the phone to me.____ She said she'd al - ways been a

danc - er, ___ She worked at fif-teen clubs a day.____

And though she thought I knew the an - swer; __ Well, I knew what I could not say. __

And so I quit the P'lice De - part - ment,__ And got my - self a stead -y

She Loves You

Moderately

loves you   and you know that can't be bad.

Yes, she

loves you   and you know you should be glad.

She

said you   hurt her so,___   She | al - most   lost   her | mind.___   But
know it's   up to you,___   I | think it's   on - ly | fair.___

now she says she knows___   You're | not the hurt - ing | kind.___   She says she⎫
Pride can hurt you too___   A - | pol - o - gize to | her___   Be - cause she⎭

225

She's Leaving Home

226

Stepping out - side she is free.
How could she do this to me?"

She _____ is
She _____ is

(We gave her most of our ___ lives
(We nev - er thought of our - selves.

leav - ing _____
leav - ing _____

Sac - ri - ficed most of our ___ lives ___
Nev - er a thought for our - selves ___

228

230

Strawberry Fields Forever

233

New York Times

"The way things are going they're gonna crucify me"

The Ballad Of John & Yoko

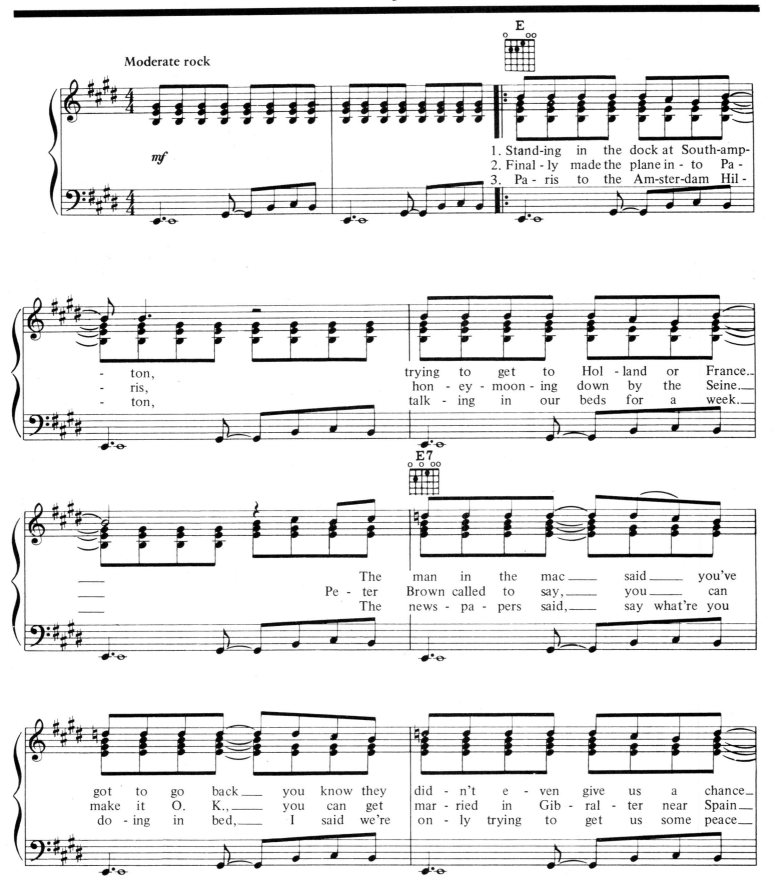

rain - y day, ___ giv- ing all your clothes to char - i -

ty. Last night the wife said, Oh boy, when you're dead you

B7

don't take noth- ing with you but your soul _____ Think!

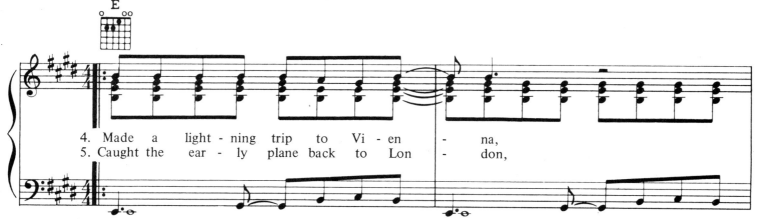

E

4. Made a light- ning trip to Vi - en - na,
5. Caught the ear - ly plane back to Lon - don,

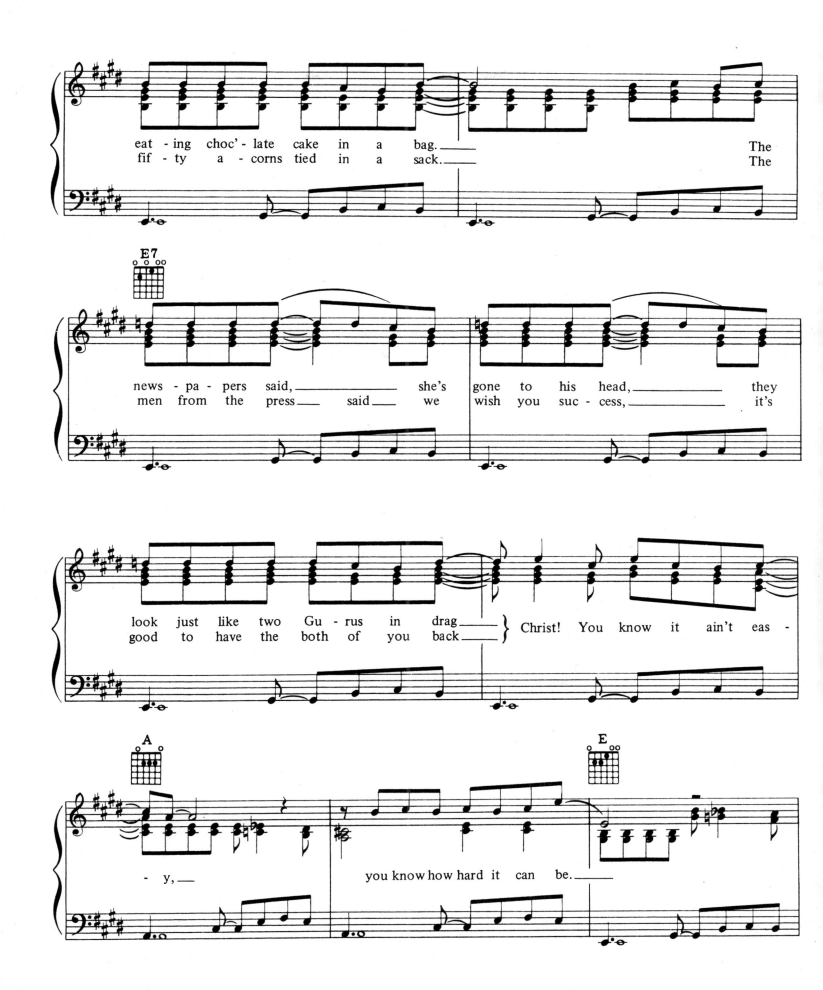

eat - ing choc' - late cake in a bag._____ The
fif - ty a - corns tied in a sack._____ The

news - pa - pers said,_____ she's gone to his head,_____ they
men from the press__ said__ we wish you suc - cess,_____ it's

look just like two Gu - rus in drag_____ } Christ! You know it ain't eas -
good to have the both of you back_____

- y, __ you know how hard it can be._____

The way things are go - ing— they're going to cru - ci - fy— me.

The way things are go - ing— they're going to cru-ci -fy— me.

The Fool On The Hill

* Guitarists tune low string to D.

go - ing down ___ And the eyes ___ in his head ___ see the world

spin - ning 'round. ___

(Piano Solo)

No - bod - y seems to like _ him, They can tell what he wants _ to do, _____ And
He nev - er lis - tens to _ them He knows that they're _ the fools, _____

he nev - er shows his feel - ings,
They don't like _ him, } But the fool _____ on the hill _____ sees the sun _____

_____ go - ing down _____ And the eyes _____ in his head _____ see the world _____

After repeat
D.S. and fade

_____ spin - ning 'round. _____

Things We Said Today

lone - ly ____ wish - ing you weren't so far a - way, ____
dream - ing ____ deep in love, not a lot to say, ____

Then I will re - mem - ber ____ things we said to - day.
Then we will re - mem - ber ____ things we said to - day.

Me, I'm just ____ the luck - y kind, ____ Love to hear ____ you say ____

that love is love. ___ And though we may ___ be blind, ___

Love is here ___ to stay ___ and that's e - nough ___ to make you mine ___

girl, ___ be the on - ly one. ___

Love me all the time, ___ girl, ___ we'll go on and on. ___

Ticket To Ride

to Coda

think twice, she ought-ta do right by me. Be - fore she gets to say - ing good-bye,

she ought-ta think twice, she ought-ta do right by me.

D.S. al Coda

1. 2.

She I

Coda

Repeat and fade

My ba-by don't care.

The Long And Winding Road

The long and wind-ing road___ that___ leads___ to your door.___
wild and wind-y night___ that the rain___ washed a - way___

will nev-er dis-ap-pear,
has left a pool of tears

I've seen that road be-fore,___ It al-ways leads___
cry-ing for the day,___ Why leave me stand-ing.

___ me here,
here,___

lead me to your___ door. The
let me know the___

*Guitarists capo up 3 frets.

252

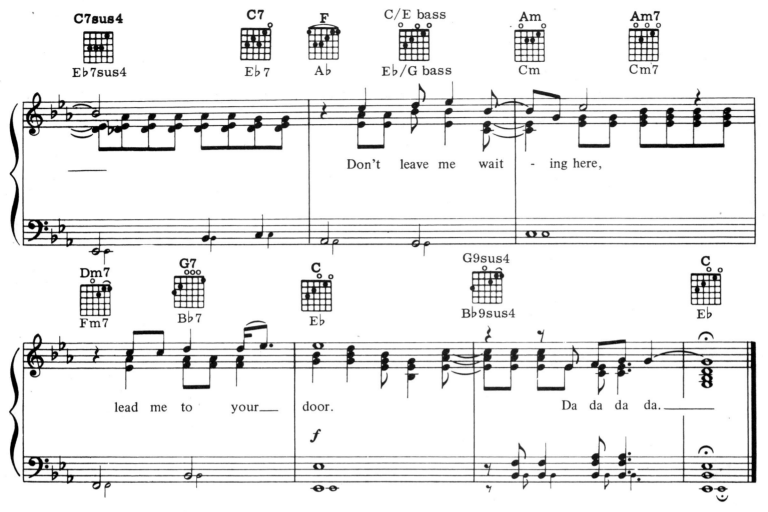

Don't leave me wait - ing here, lead me to your___ door. Da da da da.___

New York Times

When I'm Sixty-Four

quar - ter to three___ would you lock the door___
dig - ging the weeds___ who could ask for more___
fill in a form___ mine for - ev - er more___

Will you still need___ me, will you still feed___ me when I'm six - ty

four.

Oo___

You'll be

Ev - 'ry sum - mer we can rent a cot - tage in the Isle of Wight if it's not too dear.

We shall scrimp and

save;

Grand - chil - dren on your knee:

Ve - ra, Chuck and

Tacet

Dave.

D.S. al Coda

Coda

Tacet al fine

Four. Ho!

259

We Can Work It Out

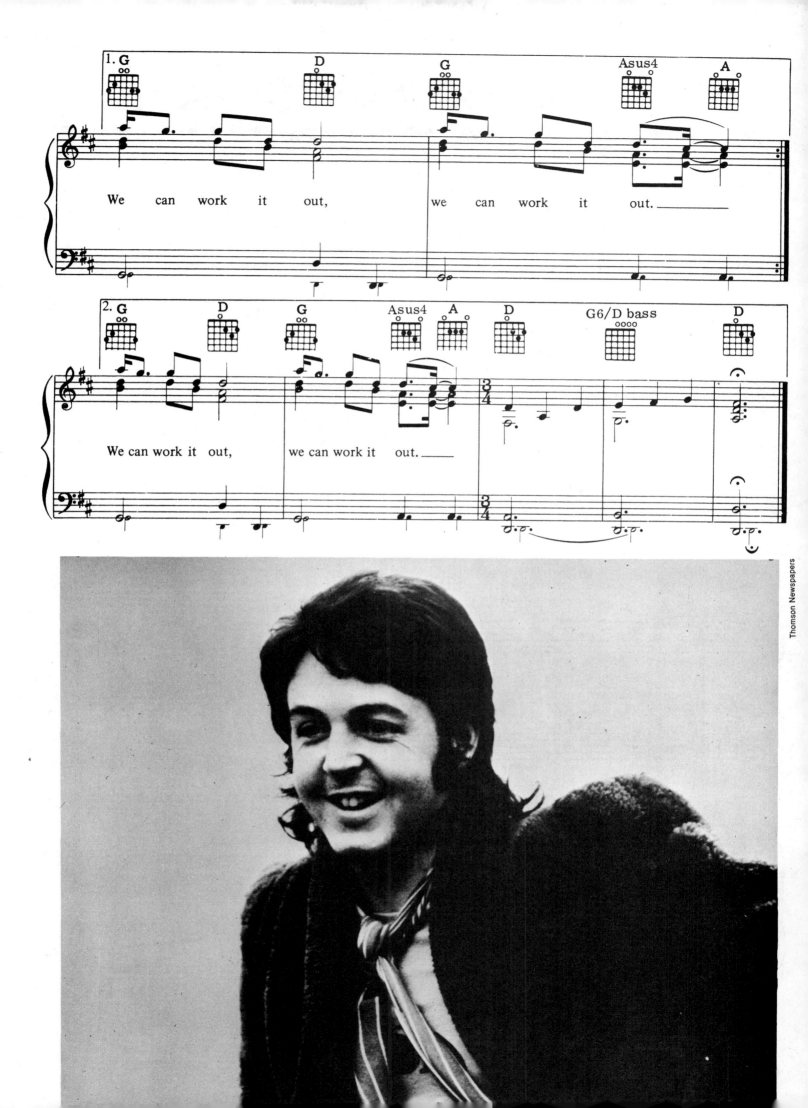

With A Little Help From My Friends

Lend me your ears___ and I'll sing___ you a song___ and I'll try___
How do I feel___ by the end___ of the day___ (are you sad
(What do you see___ when you turn___ out the light?)___ I can't tell

___ not to sing___ out of key___ Oh)
___ be - cause you're___ on your own___ No} I get by___
___ you but I know___ it's mine___ Oh)

___ with a lit - tle help___ from my friends___ Mm, I get high___

___ with a lit - tle help___ from my friends___ {Mm I'm gon - na try___
                                                 {Oh I'm gon - na try___

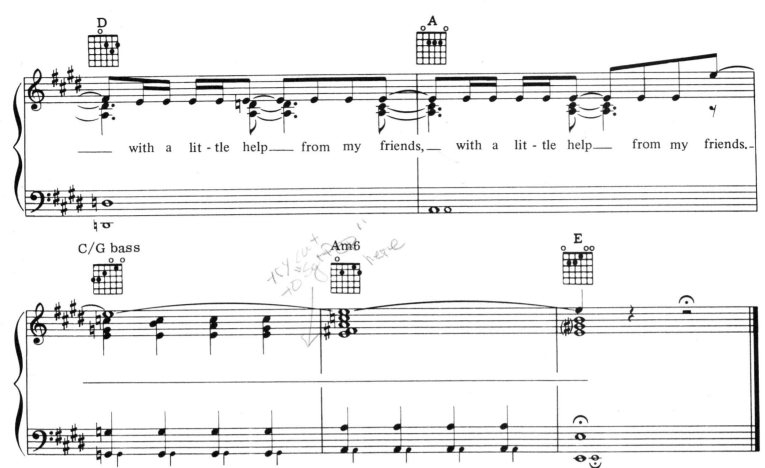

with a lit-tle help___ from my friends,___ with a lit-tle help___ from my friends.___

John in *How I Won The War*.

World Without Love

1.

C   Ab 4 fr.   G 3fr   **2.** C

love.   love.

C7   Fm   C

So I wait and in a while—   I will see my

Fm   Dm7

true love smile.—   She may come, I   know not when,—   when she does I'll

Ab 4 fr.   G 3fr   C   E7   Am   Am/Gbass

know. So ba - by, un - til   then,   lock me a - way—   And   don't al - low the—

270

Yellow Submarine

Chorus:

lived _____ be-neath the waves in our yel - low sub -ma - rine.

We all live in a yel -low sub -ma - rine, yel - low sub -ma - rine,

yel -low sub -ma - rine. We all live in a yel -low sub -ma - rine,

yel - low sub -ma - rine, yel -low sub -ma - rine. {And our friends _____ are all on
As we live _____ a life of

Yesterday

At the Watergate hearings. (6/73)

You Never Give Me Your Money

One sweet dream _____ came true _____ to - day, _____

came true _____ to - day, _____ came true _____

to - day. _____

Repeat and fade

One, two, three, four, five, six, sev - en, All good chil - dren go to heav - en.

You've Got To Hide Your Love Away

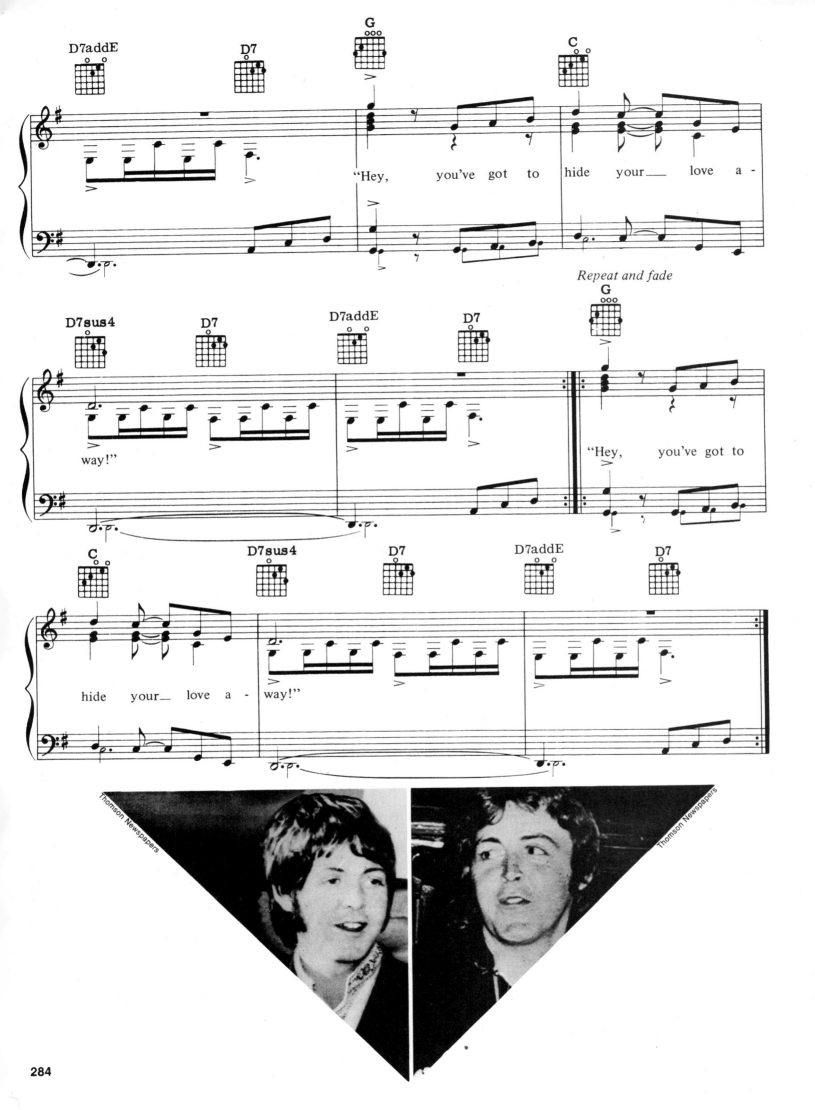

Your Mother Should Know

your moth-er should know,___ your moth-er should know.

Your moth-er should know,___

your moth-er should know.___

Your moth-er should know,___ your moth-er should know.___

Milton Okun, born in New York City, has worked in most areas of the music field—record producing, arranging, and conducting. He received his B.S. in Music Education from New York University and his Master of Education from the Oberlin Conservatory of Music, and subsequently taught music in the New York City public school system.

He was the arranger and conductor for Harry Belafonte, and the arranger and producer for Peter, Paul, and Mary during their ten-year career together. Currently he is the musical director and producer for both John Denver and the Starland Vocal Band. Milton Okun has earned forty-six gold and platinum records.

As Editor, Mr. Okun's books include:
- SOMETHING TO SING ABOUT
- New York Times, GREAT SONGS OF THE SIXTIES, VOLUMES I and II
- New York Times GREAT SONGS OF LENNON AND McCARTNEY
- New York Times COUNTRY MUSIC'S GREATEST SONGS
- New York Times GREAT SONGS OF THE SEVENTIES
- New York Times GREAT SONGS OF ABBA

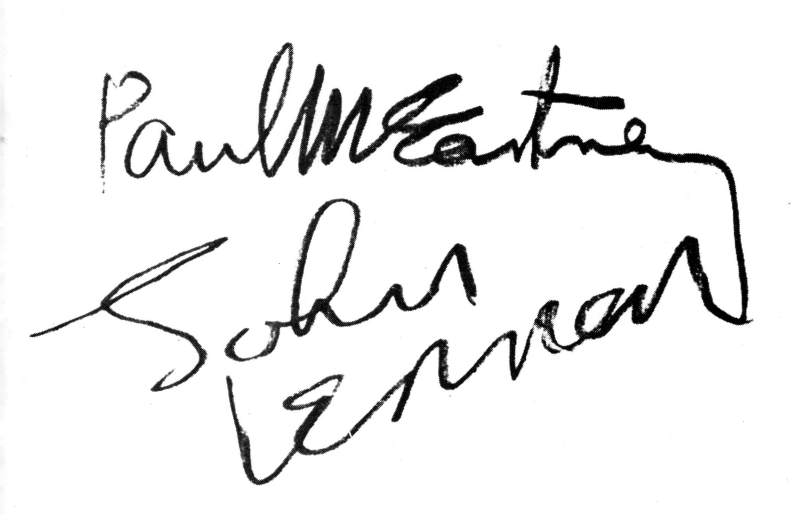